MS 1464trip/15000 words

I0132496

# The 1957 Sachs Arctic Expedition
A memoir

# Harley L. Sachs

Copyright © 2005 Harley L. Sachs
Published by IDEVCO Intellectual Properties, The
Idea Development Company. All rights reserved.

ISBN 9781939224

*Books by Harley L. Sachs:*

*Novels*

*Queer Company*
*Never Trust a Talking Horse*
*The Gold Chromosome*
*Murder by Mail (Scratch—out!)!*
*Ben Zakkai's Coffin*
*The Search for Jesse Bram*
*The Mystery Club Solves a Murder*
*The Mystery Club and the Dead Doctor*
*The Mystery Club and the Hidden Witness*
*The Mystery Club and the Serial Widow*
*Deliver me From Evil*
*White Slave*
*Conspiracy!*
*Murder in the Keweenaw*
*The Lollipop Murder*
*Betrayal*
*Retribution*
*Burnt Out*
*Sam in Love*

*Collections of short fiction*

*Ahoy! Quarterdeck! (Irma Quarterdeck Reports)*
*Anna-Lena's Troll and other stories*
*Threads of the Covenant: The Jews of Red Jacket*
*Misplaced Persons*

*Non-Fiction*

*Freelance Non-Fiction Articles*
*The Misadventures of Cpl. Sachs*
*The 1957 Sachs Arctic Expedition*
*From Tent to Castle: Memoir of a Year-Long Honeymoon*
*IS*
*Chilly-Chilly BANG! How We Freelanced Through Europe's Coldest Winter in a VW with a Kid*
*Essays and Columns: 1992-2011*
*The Writing Life*

*Cartoons*

*Hunting the Mail Buoy and other hazards to navigation*

**Preamble**

Hitchhiking. In 1949, before the network of interstate freeways was built, it was still common to see hitchhikers. Indiana University's main campus in Bloomington, Indiana was 185 miles south of my home in South Bend, a straight shot, at least as far as Indianapolis, on US 31. I didn't own a car. If I couldn't find a ride with someone who owned one and would accept a few bucks for gas, my alternative was to hitchhike. I soon learned the techniques of being successful: never wear sunglasses that hid your eyes, always smile, carry a suitcase, look respectable, and most important, hold up a sign showing your destination.

Where you stand is important. Intersections are best, for people slow down. At night it's vital to be in a well-lit place, not standing in the dark in some deserted spot at the side of the road. It's best not to be out on the highway where drivers have picked up speed. At sixty miles an hour, a speeding motorist has only a few seconds to see you, make eye contact and decide to stop or pass you by. It's too dangerous to slam on the brakes at that speed.

The right psychological effect was important. A sign with a distant destination might be ignored by someone going only a short distance, but it might also catch a driver going where you wanted to go, even if it were hundreds of miles and days away. In time, having been caught in rain that turned my cardboard signs to a soggy mess, I made an all-purpose sign out of an old white sheet I tucked around one side of the suitcase. For the right psychological effect the destination, heavily marked in black crayon, said simply "home". Who wouldn't give someone a lift so he could get home?

After graduation from Indiana University and service in the US Army in Heidelberg, Germany, I returned to I.U. and earned a Master's degree but was not ready to look for a job. I had never had a real job. You could hardly call my army experience as an unwilling draftee a career, but on a formula of a day and a half of school for every day in the army I had accrued at least two, maybe three more years of GI Bill. Until that ran out I could be a career student. Not only that, but I could do it in Europe, my own version of what the British once called "the grand tour."

There was precedent. Learning that European professors never took attendance, Art Buchwald had done it in Paris, writing restaurant reviews for the Herald Tribune when the GI Bill ran out. When Buchwald ran out of restaurants in Paris, he shifted to wineries. That launched his successful journalism career. I had majored in Creative Writing at I.U. Following Art Buchwald's Paris example, I decided to return to Europe to live on government checks while writing a novel or two and taking courses at the University of Stockholm, Sweden and the International Graduate School.

Cashing in my meager savings and what remained of my GI separation pay, I had just enough money for a one way, eight day tourist class passage on the Kungsholm from New York to Gothenberg. Whatever was left over had to last me until the first GI Bill check came in from the headquarters in Paris. After that? Who knew?

The GI Bill paid only for the eight months of the school year. I did not have a work permit, so couldn't get a regular job in Stockholm. I did pick up a little extra money as a schlepper at the twice annual mink auctions, carrying up to five thousand bundles of mink pelts for buyers to inspect. I had also sold a couple of freelance magazine articles, my first professional sales, thanks to my old army buddy Richard Ziff who was editor of several automotive magazines at Great American Publications in New York. Those few sales were not enough to pay rent for a room.

Housing was strictly controlled in Stockholm. The digs the secretary at the International Graduate School had found for me in the apartment of Mrs. Eklund, a single mother and her son in the Bromma suburb, were no longer available even if I could afford the rent. Mrs. Eklund was moving having successfully traded her suburb apartment for one more desirable. When the school term ended I was effectively homeless.

Ah, well, not to worry. I had more affluent friends I could crash with for a week or two at a time. American Express provided free mail services for tourists, so I had an address: c/o Amexco, Stockholm, Sweden. If I husbanded my meager cash carefully I should make it until September when the GI Bill kicked in again. I looked upon the months of European summer as an opportunity to travel on the cheap.

This was the time of life to do it. I was twenty-six and single. Later I would probably have a wife, a family, and a job. For now, I could go where my thumb could carry me on my meager savings. Though inexpensive, even the price of youth hostels was out of the question and one could stay in them only a few days at a time. Instead, I'd live in a tent and hitchhike.

But where to? My army travels, done with an Army ID card, no passport, had been south of Scandinavia. With the International Graduate School students I had made a trip to Helsinki, Finland. I had not been to Norway.

Stockholm in summer has an aura of enchantment. It is almost never dark. It is a magical time of the year. At midnight enough light remains to read a newspaper out of doors. On June 21st, the summer solstice, the Swedes celebrate the long twilight with parties like the one in Strindberg's "Miss Julie." In that famous play, in a kind of enchanted pagan orgy, Miss Julie goes to bed with her partner at the last dance. That was not my experience. That was probably just as well, for the experience was so unnerving for the independent heroine of the play that she kills herself.

Stockholm's not being quite dark even at midnight was not the same as continuous, bright daylight. What did intrigue me was to experience the midnight sun. Though it's never quite dark at the Stockholm summer solstice, to see the midnight sun you must be above the arctic circle. June 21st was already past, so the sun would be at even higher latitudes. I would have to travel farther north than the Arctic circle.

Looking at the map of Scandinavia I saw that the northernmost point of land in Europe is North Cape, Norway. Would it be possible to hitchhike to North Cape? What an adventure that would be!

A classmate at the International Graduate School agreed to go with me. We would split the cost of a small tent and head to the far north. Alas, the summer solstice may have been my friend's downfall. He wasn't going. He announced that he was in love and would I please buy his half interest in the tent?

That was a disappointing setback. I hadn't hitchhiked yet in Europe. In the Army I had always taken the trains at half fare, or ridden with friends. I was uncertain. My Swedish after two semesters was rudimentary. In conversations I often ran out of words and, lacking the right word, had to figure out convoluted ways to express something that would be simple if I only knew the right vocabulary. It helped that I knew some German, but in spite of multi-lingual public education, not everyone in Sweden knew English or German. As for Norwegian, that was a total mystery to me.

Travel alone is not as much fun as travel with someone. Experiences are best when shared. If one traveler is at a loss for ideas, a companion may come up with something, notice a landmark, ask a question. Of course, there can be downsides if the companion is never satisfied, had interests in direct conflict, has more money to spend, wants to eat in expensive restaurants, stay in nice hotels, get up when you want to sleep in, won't do his or her share of the work, etc.

They say the best crew on a small boat is a married couple and that a crew of three is the worst for two gang up on the third. With those negatives to consider, there is something to be said for doing it alone.

When I told my Swedish friend Sven Huldt that I planned to hitchhike to North Cape he said he didn't think there was a road. It was fjord country, mountainous, a wild and forbidding arctic landscape.

I learned that during World War II the German occupying army had built a strategic road up the coast of Norway. I found a brochure "Med bil til Nordkapp" which described the journey by car. It might be rough, but it was possible.

All the more reason to try for it. If I ran out of road, I could simply turn back. Whatever happened, it would be an adventure and better than imposing on the hospitality of friends who had to put me up during the summer while I had nothing but an American Express address.

Though my original companion had backed out, my travel plans intrigued another couple, Jay and Lil Hutchinson. They were both Americans, newlyweds who were fellow classmates at the International Graduate School. We studied the map of Scandinavia. They agreed to meet me at Russenes, the jumping off port for Honningsvåg, the Arctic port closest to North Cape.

Jay and Lil would hitchhike, too, but while I went west to Norway and then north, they would go north though Sweden and East through Finland. We would rendezvous about July 7 or 8, so if I left on July 1 I had a week to make it all the way up the rugged coast of Norway to the farthest north of the Scandinavian Arctic.

I prepared. In spite of having been a Boy Scout (one overnight in a pup tent), and in the US Army (one night on an alert in a tent made of two GI shelter halves) I was never a camper. On that Boy Scout outing we had attempted to bake bread on a stick over a campfire. The result was sticky dough with a burnt outer crust. I had tried to sleep one night on a Lake Michigan beach and found sand mighty uncomfortable. My outdoor experience was otherwise nil.

I now had a tent. I had a sporting good store make up a fly sheet to fit over it. I still had my old Boy Scout knapsack, a crude affair with simple straps that cut into the shoulders. At a sporting goods store I bought a used frame for the pack and laboriously stitched on the leather attachment. I would also need to cook my meals.

While stationed in Heidelberg I had bought a tiny German camp stove, basically a gasoline blow torch, no bigger than a family size can of Campbell's soup. This was the sort of gasoline stove American GI's plundered off the bodies of dead German soldiers during World War II. The German stove was far lighter and more convenient than the heavy Coleman stoves that required white gasoline. My German stove used ordinary regular gas. I had my Boy Scout canteen.

On discharge from the US Army I had "liberated" two superannuated, crude GI sleeping bags, mummy style, a simple wool liner and a poplin cotton cover. I opened the side seams and sewed the two into a double sleeping bag. Perhaps I would find someone to share it with. After all, this was Scandinavia. Perhaps I would find my own Miss Julie.

To complete the outfit I went to a camping store and bought a set of nesting cookware--a frying pan that fit outside a two liter pot and a smaller one liter, all with folding handles and lids. I added a plastic cup, small Thermos bottle, knife, fork, and spoon and a six inch hunting knife in a sheath. A couple of aluminum serving dishes, handles removed, would serve either as plates or soup bowls.

Using my pocket knife I scratched the words "Sachs Arctic Expedition, 1957" into the two pot lids. I was ready.

## Day One: Monday, July 1, 1957

I had other baggage that had to stay behind. I had left the United States with all my worldly goods, saying goodbye to my parents and brothers in South Bend, Indiana and leaving for who knew how long. My personal effects, books, tape recorder, typewriter, etc. were all packed into a cubic meter wooden crate the army had used when I shipped home from Heidelberg to Indiana. It was so heavy that only professional movers with lifting straps could shift it. That sturdy crate had served me well and was stored with the friend who'd backed out of the North Cape trip. After all, since he'd let me down and decided not to make the trip, the least he could do was let me park my huge crate in his room, right?

What was left for my adventure to the Arctic were a minimal wardrobe, a spare pair of GI khaki pants, my army issue olive drab towel, a sweater, a light jacket, GI raincoat and whatever toiletries, underwear and socks could be crammed into the small Boy Scout knapsack.

True to my hitchhiking form learned in the days at Indiana University, I made up a cardboard sign that said "Nord Kapp." That was so far away that it should intrigue curious drivers.

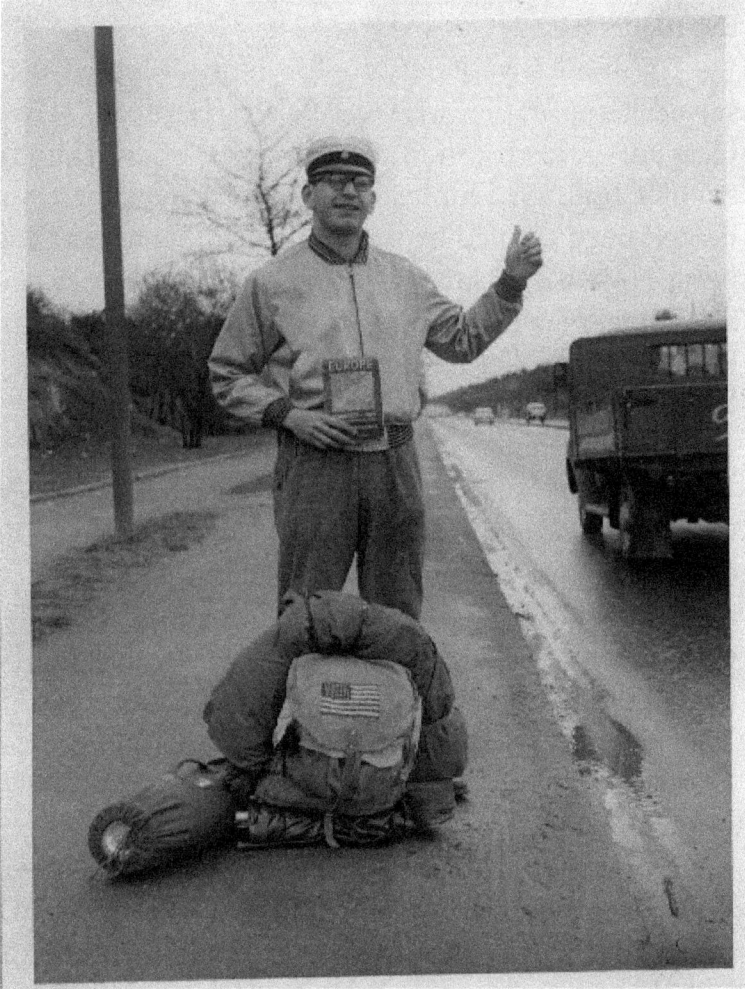

I also had sewn an American flag on the flap of my knapsack, so drivers would know I was American. I topped off my outfit with a white Swedish student cap, the uniform of someone who has passed the university matriculation exams. In a glance someone could see that I was American, a student, destination North Cape, certainly someone interesting.

Having minored in German at IU, spent over a year in Heidelberg, and studied Swedish for a year in

Stockholm, I had enough linguistic skills to communicate with almost anyone I would meet on the road.

Up until my departure for North Cape I had stayed temporarily with a Welsh classmate, Tony Heaven, in his room in the University of Stockholm student housing Domus. Tony was a nice chap but he had been spoiled by two maiden aunts who raised him. They took care of all his needs, so he lacked discipline, never picked up after himself, and without his aunts to look after him was just short of slovenly. Fortunately at Domus he had a spare bed.

The morning of my departure arrived, July 1, 1957. Tony was a late sleeper and barely stirred when I left Domus at 6:00 AM. The morning was cool and I was anxious to get on the road. In the cool morning air I boarded a Stockholm bus that took me to the edge of the city. According to my map, I would travel west toward Norway on the E3. The route went through Södertälje to Örebro and Eskilstuna.

Standing at the side of the road and hoping for a ride, there is anticipation, excitement and adventure. Will someone stop? Who will it be? Will they take you a mile down the road or a hundred miles? Or will they drop you at a deserted crossroad in the middle of nowhere in the rain, at night?

I had had such a traumatic experience. Hitchhiking back to boot camp while in the Army, I was dropped on a pitch dark night at 11:00 PM in central Illinois, six hours away from reveille. If I did not make it back to Camp Breckinridge, Kentucky by 5:30 AM I would be AWOL and subject to court martial. My pass was only good for fifty miles from the camp and I had traveled hundreds. Fearing the worst, I stood in my uniform on the deserted, dark highway. At that hour there was no traffic. I was most certainly doomed.

Within minutes, the very first car stopped: it was another GI headed for the same camp. We were back by 5 AM. Sometimes you get lucky, really lucky.

That's part of the excitement. As long as the rides keep coming, hitchhiking is usually fun. Of course, asking for a free ride someplace, one is a beggar, but the driver is getting something in return: relief from boredom, companionship, a good story, sometimes even someone who help with the driving. It's been my experience that, with few exceptions, only nice people pick you up. They are generous enough to share their space and trusting enough to let a stranger into their vehicle. You have to look like an interesting person they'd like to share their space with for a few miles.

If there is danger, is it usually if the driver is careless, speeds, or is even drunk. I once got a lift in Southern Michigan with two drunken painters driving a speedy Hudson Hornet. They were carrying a refrigerator behind them in the back seat. I squeezed in front in the notorious death seat. This was before seat belts or air bags. In a collision, unprotected by the steering wheel, a person sitting in the passenger seat would either go through the windshield or merely get a fatal concussion while breaking the glass with his head. If we had hit anything at 94 miles an hour, we would have been crushed between the engine in front and the refrigerator in the back. I was glad to get out of that one unscathed.

Leaving Stockholm so early on that first day, before shops were open, I had no chance to buy food for the trip to North Cape. Somewhere along the line I would have to buy some tea bags, bread, margarine, jam, cheese, and maybe a bit of hard salami that didn't require refrigeration.

In 1957, Swedes still drove on the left side of the road, the only European country besides Great Britain that didn't have right hand traffic. In a southern suburb of Stockholm I parked myself at the left side of the road and stuck out my thumb. I had a very long trip ahead of me. Looking at that prodigious and intimidating map of Scandinavia, my first day's goal was to make it to the Norwegian border.

It's there that the white lines in the road funneled traffic from the left side to the right, Norwegian side. It was such a frequent cause of accidents that the Swedes eventually decided to follow the rest of continental Europe. On H day, the H standing for Höger (Right), in one weekend all the bus stops, trolley stops, traffic lights, and signs were changed. In one tense weekend, Swedes changed from drivers on the left to drivers on the right. Today the chief traffic problem is with Norwegians who cross into Sweden north of Gothenberg, break the speed limit, and burden the National Health hospitals with the expense of treating all those foreign victims of accidents.

It didn't take long for me to get to Södertalje, but I was stuck for an hour before I could get farther. Eventually, on the first day, I made it across that peculiar, lane-switch at the Swedish-Norwegian border. I hoped to add another stamp to my new passport, but one within Scandinavia, the Nordic Union, border crossings were perfunctory. No stamp.

My last ride of the day was with a friendly Norwegian couple who gave me their copy of their auto club Norwegian road guide. It was my first exposure to the Norwegian language and I could puzzle through most of it. There were differences in spelling and not all words were the same in both languages, but my Swedish and German made the touring book intelligible. The guide book confirmed the existence of the road to the far north. Where fjiords blocked the way, there were ferry connections.

I arrived dead tired just across the border in Kongsvinger, Norway and looked for a place for the night. Sven Huldt had told me about the Scandinavian Gypsy law. You may pitch a tent for twenty-four hours anywhere out of sight of a house as long as you are gone the next day and do no damage to crops or property. Unlike the United States where property is fenced and posted with "No Trespassing" and "Keep Out" signs, Scandinavia was open. I did not have to find an official camp ground. I just needed a secluded spot.

Before I left Stockhoolm I had stood on a coin operated scale and weighed myself with the loaded back pack. So laden, I was 253 pounds, so my gear weighed more than sixty pounds. In the army I had never been able to shoulder my duffle bag and carry it more than a few feet. I could barely get the pack on my shoulders, much less carry it and the tent. Not far from a Kongsvinger highway bridge, beside a river, I pitched my tent for the first night of my expedition.

The mosquitoes were fierce. I was having my first taste of what drives the caribo mad. Putting up a tent without letting the mosquitoes in takes some finesse, skill, and timing. At least my tent had a floor and a screened vent at the back. I also had a fly sheet, a necessity I'd read about. Without a fly sheet, a canvas tent in the rain, touched on the inside, will leak.

By the time I got the tent up, unwilling to fool with the gasoline stove while being tormented by mosquitoes, I simply made a couple of sandwiches and crawled into that primitive sleeping bag, exhausted.

I was only a few miles from Oslo, but my route would turn north before that. My goal the next day, if I could make it, would be Trondheim where Ibsen had his first job as a theater manager. It was a long way up the Atlantic coast. After Trondheim, how much traffic could there possibly be?

## Day two: Tuesday, July 2, 1957

An old travel advertisement had the slogan "Getting there is half the fun." That's not true. If life is a journey, "there" is death, the end of the trip, the end of everything. Looking at it that way, the trip is all of the fun, for unless you ascribe to some idea of paradise, at the end of life's travel there is nothing. The act of traveling is itself the whole reward.

What do travelers generally talk about? When they come home from Europe they have a collection of photographs of themselves in various places, places they can no longer remember. "Here I am in front of some church, but I don't remember what country it's in." If an army travels on its stomach, as Napoleon was supposed to have said, some tourists travel with their mouths. They remember restaurants and meals, the tastes, the recipes, the prices, the service. Some finicky American travelers with sensitive stomachs or fear of mysterious foods carry tins of tuna in their baggage.

Other travelers talk about the accomodation, the hotels, the rooms, whether the beds were comfortable. Americans talk about the toilet paper, the slick single sheets in Scandinavia, the rough sandpaper of Germany. Some Americans with discriminating bottoms carry their own. If they frequented hostels, they talk about which was best and whether others in the hostel were friendly or might steal.

The best traveler does homework first, reads up in the guidebooks, knows the landmarks, what to see in the museums, the history of the place, the featrures that make each destination unique. Unfortunately, I had no such knowledge. Except for my remote destination, I had little clue of what I might expect to see.

Art Buchwald said of Americans visiting the Louvre in Paris that it was possible to run through the place, see Winged Victory, the Venus de Milo, and the Mona Lisa in three minutes flat thereby missing all that other stuff. Is this the way to travel?

At least in 1957 Europe had not yet been invaded by Macdonald's, Kentucky Fried Chicken, or Pizza Hut, those fast food joints that permit Americans to travel abroad but remain in familiar territory, not to experience the culture shock of a continental breakfast.

But what about me? What about a hitchhiker's experience of travel? Not staying in hotels or eating in restaurants, confined to eating light weight food that could be carried in a backpack without spoiling, I wouldn't be able to report on some five star restaurant or hotel. I even carried my own toilet paper in case of the necesssity of a dump in the woods.

An ideal traveler who explores the fascinating world around him isn't worried about timetables or destinations. Whim carries him. Chance takes him to some surprise. That was why, traveling on a three day pass from Heidelberg to Venice and Florence with fellow GI Lenny Rozansky, we explored the Grand Canal and the Lido but never saw St. Mark's Square. We were able to talk about the cheap hotel room and the souvenir bed bug bites we left with. How much can you cram into a three day pass?

What kind of travel experience, then, is the Sachs Arctic Expedition dash to North Cape? Did Scott, in his dash for the South Pole, do anything but try to endure the journey, so many miles a day, suffering only the cold and ice before he froze to death on the way back? His timetable was limited by his own endurance and supply of food and fuel. For me, it was making it to Russenes in time to meet Jay and Lil and see the midnight sun at the most nothern part of Europe.

The first day I had traveled almost due west from Stockholm and, two weeks after the summer solstice, it got almost dark.  At least, inside my dark green tent it was dark enough to sleep. The further north I traveled, the closer I would be to twenty-four hours of daylight.

I had a sheet of plastic spread underneath the tent floor to hold out the damp. I did not carry an air mattress or even a piece of closed cell foam for a sleeping pad. Ground was ground. If I could sleep on the floor of a friend's place in Stockholm, I could sleep on the ground in the forest, as long as I had first cleared away stones and sticks.

If you are tired enough, you can sleep anywhere. In basic training I had mastered the art of falling asleep in a few minutes wherever I was, even on sharp gravel.

Goal for the second day was Trondheim. The first morning traffic on the road nearby woke me up. In the early Tuesday morning light of Kongsvinger I packed. I knew that a wet canvas tent was not only subject to rot but was heavy, so I was careful to take the tent down and roll it up on the plastic to keep it clean. If it wasn't rolled tightly I could not stuff it in its bag and leave room in the same sack for the nested pots and pan. The old army sleeping bag was rolled into a sausage and tied over the top of my back pack. I struggled to get it on my shoulders and walked to the highway.

I had a slow start. I made very slow progress toward Hamar, Norway. Seeing my sign, drivers always asked in astonishment "Skal i heijke til nortdkapp?" Will you hitchhike to North Cape? I was clearly someone awesome or crazy, an adventurer.

I was also picking up the Norwegian lilt. My beginner's Swedish was spoken in the middle of the mouth. German was more gutteral and down on the tongue. Norwegian was more nasal and high pitched. With practice, my Swedish with my version of a Norwegian accent, I could fake Norwegian for a minute of two before my brains hit gridlock.

One driver, a salesman, commiserated with me about the mosquitoes that had driven me into my tent the night before without waiting to cook a meal on the gasoline stove. He generously gave me a stick of mosquito repellant, something I had failed to pack when assembling pots and pan and other utensils. Anyone traveling in the far north must be prepared with bug dope.

At a small village where I was stuck waiting for a ride for over an hour, I got a lesson in the best hitchhiking combination: a guy and a girl. A girl hitchhiking alone could be in danger. A guy hitchhiking alone could be dangerous. A couple hitchhiking together could be romantic. While I stood with my student hat, American flag, and sign and didn't get a ride, a young couple got a lift almost immediately. Next time I set off one one of these trips it would help if I had a girl with me. Romantic or not, it would help at getting a lift.

I already had such a plan. One of my Stockholm pals, Ingrid Henning, planned to hitchhike with me to Paris after my North Cape adventure. I would meet her and her family in Härnosand on my way back to Stockholm.

Finally I got picked up by a Norewegian who took me all the way to Lillehamar, famous for winter skiing. Of course, this was July and there was no snow in Lillehamar. But it's a small world after all as they say in Disneyland. The Norwegian who picked me up for that leg of the journey had lived in my home town, South Bend, Indiana! Not being in the market for a fur coat at the time, he didn't know my parents' store, but it was amazing to meet someone with South Bend, Indiana as a common denominator. That's the real adventure of hitchhiking--the people you meet.

People like it when you show an interest in them. When hitching to college and back I always asked the drivers about their jobs and their lives. I'd met many interesting people. Once it was a condom salesman whose outrageous stories have provided me with tales to re-tell for years since. Once, seeing chains on the floor of the back seat I thought the driver was in the hardware business, but they were manacles. He was an FBI agent  picking up a prisoner and took me along to see what it was like. It was an experience no ordinary traveler would have had--unless, perhaps, if they were arrested for vagrancy.

When I arrived at  Lillehamar it was already 5:30 in the afternoon and I was about to give it up for the day. I had been on the road about twelve hours after not very much sleep on the ground in Kongsvinger. Then I got lucky again. A German writer from Hamburg whose wife worked as a nurse in Mosjoen, much farther north, pulled up in a new Fiat. He was in a hurry to be reunited with her and drove fast.

North of Lilllehamar, which is ski country, the landscape grew more and more breathtaking. This was the Norway so often depicted in tourist brochure photographs. Rugged mountains with snow in July, deep valleys and fjords were sights that soon satiated the eyes. That is, if you could take the time to look at scenery and not watch for the next hair-raising curve in the road.. The road was now paved only in populated places. The German driver, used to roaring flat out on the autobahn, pressed the Fiat to the limits of roadworthiness. He was skillful, but how long could he keep it up? He'd been driving since Hamburg with hardly a break.

I was always fascinated by how architecture changed when you crossed a border. In the army I had visited   Germany, Denmark, Switzerland, France, Luxembourg, England, Italy, and Holland, and noted how building styles differed-- tile roofs in Germany, corrugated Tetanit in Denmark, thatched roofs in Holland, and so on, each adding to the cultural flavor of the place.

South of Trondheim, Norway I saw sod roofs on some huts, something I'd heard about but never seen. One such building actually had a couple of small trees growing out of the roof and a goat grazing on the gress. I wondered how such buildings could keep out the rain in such a wet climate. Those didn't look like dwellings, but might be above ground root cellars, an insulated place to store vegetables if the ground was all rock and digging a cellar impossible.

I was now in snow country even in July. In the distance on the hilltops snow still lingered though it was July. I would soon be in the Arctic.

Most cities of the world have grown up along trade routes, seaports and rivers. The E3 to the north of Norway follows the coastline. Norway, warmed by the Gulf Stream, is a rainy place. The windshield wipers of the Fiat beat a steady thump-thump that mesmerized the eyes. The roar of the tires on the gravel was monotonous. The German driver was tired, having driven all the way from Hamburg. I was afraid he would fall asleep, miss a corve, and we would plunge over a cliff into the sea. It was pouring rain as we reached Trondheim with many kilometers yet to go before Mosjoen.

Exhausted, the driver pulled off the road outside Trondheim to sleep for a few hours in the car. I would have to get out. There was no soft flat spot to put up my tent for a few hours. In the pouring rain and grey light of the Norwegian summer night I set up the tent as quickly as I could and crawled into the sleeping bag, exhausted. It was 1:00 AM.

Germans waste no time, especially en route to a reunion with a spouse. Four hours later the toot of the Fiat's horn woke me up. The rain has diminished to a persistent, cold drizzle. I hastily broke camp and gathered my gear. We were on the road again, heading for Mosjoen.

## Day three: Wednesday, July 3, 1957

Still with the German driver in the Fiat we drove all day through little places like Levanger, Verdal, Maere, Steinkjer, Formofoss, Greng, and Namskogen, until we arrived in Mosjoen, a pretty town on Vefsna fjord. No sod roofed huts here. It was a surprisingly modern place, the buildings of painted stucco. The main street was alongside the wharf where ships were tied up. The German's wife worked at what had to be a regional hospital. I was introduced. We exchanged addresses.

Addrresses? Yes. I was establishing a pattern of sending thank-you postcards to people who gave me especially generous rides. Eventually I would make up a special personal postal card showing me in my hitchhiking outfit to send telling my hosts that I had arrived safely at whatever destination.

I was off again. By then it was 3:00 PM and I thought I might make it another 70 kilometers to Mo, just south of the Arctic Circle. I got to Mo at 7:30 PM, though you could hardly call it evening. In Stockholm in the winter the sun had gone down by 2:00 in the afternoon after a mere four hours of daylight, overcast with hardly any sunshine but now it was the Scandinavian high summer. It was never dark.

It had been a long day. I'd been on the road since five in the morning outside Trondheim with less than four hours sleep. I was ready to call it quits and search for a place to put up my tent when I got another ride. This one carried me across the Arctic Circle.

I was not properly prepared for the cold. My light jacket and a single sweater were scant

protection against the wind. If I added my raincoat it provided no warmth, just a windbreak. I had a ride in a little delivery van and asked the driver to stop at the stone marker designating the Arctic Circle so I could set up my twin lens reflex German Ikoflelx camera on its flimsy tripod and take a picture. The camera was heavy as a brick, the tripod the minimum one could possibly carry. It collapsed to about eight inches, small enough to slip into a pack

pack. I set it up and a gust of raw Arctic wind slammed the van door against the camera. I rescued it, set the manual exposure and the self timer, pressed the shutter release and hurried to the roadside marker.

It was bitterly cold and wet, a landscape of rock and snow, no trees, a truly miserable place. If this was high summer, what must winter be like? Surely the roads would then be impassible. I had made it to the Arctic! Though it had not seen it yet, I was in the land of the midnight sun. Now if I could only stop shivering…

I was let off near a little, mossy dale, a bit of woods. It was raining, not the downpour I had experienced the brief night before tenting on a bed of wet gravel outside Trondheim. The first night had been on hard ground outside Kongsvinger. Neither had been condusive to real rest.

The first night in the Arctic turned out to be the most comfortable of the entire trip. The reindeeer moss was about a foot thick, a springy, though wet mattress so deep that when I pushed my metal tent pegs into it the tent floor puffed up like it was inflated.

My German gasoline stove had a narrow range between just barely functioning and overheating until it blew the safety valve and had to be doused before it exploded. Setting the valve properly required practice and finess. For once it worked perfectly, but besides making a pot of tea with my canteen of water, what did I have to eat? Not much.

Something you see in Norway and hardly anywhere else is tomato soup sold in the shape of a large chocolate bar. Condensed to a firm paste, it's to be broken up and dissolved in hot water. Without the weight of a can or a jar, such condensed soup is perfect fare for a camper living out of a rucksack in the chilly Arctic.

I was again in luck. I had company: two Norwegian boys who were hitchiking. Would it be OK if they set up their tent nearby? Of course. With me struggling to understand their brand of Norwegian and them unaccustomed to my rudimentary Swedish, we made ourselves understood.

They lived in Kirkenes, not far from Hammarfest, Norway's equivalent of Point Barrow, Alaska, and were headed for Trondheim, which for them was the deep south. Coming from the far north they had brought with them only a sack full of deep fried fiskebullar. They had eaten nothing but fried fiskebullar, fish balls, for two days and were tired of them.

I had never eaten fiskebullar, certainly not fried. The closest I'd experienced were gefilte fish, boiled fish dumplings made of a variety of fish bound with some egg and served with horseradish at Passover. For me, fried fish balls would be a new trourist experience. I traded some of my food for a greasy paper sack with the last of their fiskebullar, heated them up in my frying pan with its folding handles. The gasoline stove hissed merrily. The fiskebullar crackled in the pan. Fiskebullar were OK, but one had to be hungry. I was.

I ate a big meal, wiped the bit of soot off the bottom of the pan and my small pot on the reindoor moss, packed up the utensils, and spread out the sleeping bag on the springy mattress of moss. It was

11 PM. In the last three nights I had slept a total of only sixteen hours. I was worn out.

Listening to the occasional drops of light rain on the tent, I discovered I had pitched the tent on a hidden stick. I curled around it and slept.

### Day Four: Thursday, the 4th of July

You might wonder how Norwegians get around without a car in the far north. It turns out that there's a bus line, the North Norway Busses on the Arctic highway. Route 9500 ran from Saldtal to Kirkenes and the busses traveled in a convoy of two or three, possibly in case one broke down. Kirkenes, on the Finnish border, was beyond Russenes, my rendesvous point where I would join Jay and Lil Hutchinson, but I was not going to buy a bus ticket. I still had time to hitchhike. I had seen the busses the day before, but had not ventured to flag one down. A hitchhiker is a hitchhiker, not a paying passenger. Except when in the middle of a city, it is a matter of pride and honor to hitch, not to wimp out and take a bus.

After leisurely breaking camp and reluctantly leaving my bed of reindeer moss (with stick), I got back on the road. The two Norwegian boys were long gone on their way south. I wasn't doing very well on my way north.

I got only ten miles and was dropped by the seaside on a totally deserted stretch of the gravel highway. Across the road was the calm Arctic sea. Beside me was a precipitous hillside. The road was gravel as rough as railway ballast. It was not actually raining, but it was cold and dead quiet. The only sound was the lapping of the waves on the stony shore and an occasional cry of a sea gull. No traffic.

I could see about two or three miles to the south as the road skirted the long, deserted Norwegian coastline. About once every half hour I would spot a vehicle appearing in the far distance. As it drew nearer, I could make out the faint sound of the engine and the tires on the gravel. At last, it would get close enough for me to stick out my hitchhiker's thumb. The vehicle, often tourists packed full of baggage with no room for anyone else, would speed by. I was stuck.

If I had to spend what passed for night in the Arctic, there was no place to pitch the tent. There was no sandy beach, no reindeer moss, no place flat. After six hours without a ride I saw the North Norway bus coming. I had no pride left to swallow, flagged it down and bought a ticket for the few miles further to Narvik. I paid the driver out of my stash of Norwegian kronor and settled down, relieved to be moving again.

Narvik is a historic seaport, the most important in northern Norway. It is in Narvik that the iron ore trains from Kiruna, on the other side of the Swedish border, deliver their valuable loads. Kiruna has one of the world's largest underground iron mines. The school there is known for its solarium, a room of special glass that lets in the sun's rays. Without sunlight for the human skin to absorb ultraviolet rays and make vitamin D, there is a serious risk of vitamin deficiency.

At the end of World War II the German navy tried to hide their ships in the Narvik fjord, but they were discovered and sunk by allied bombers. I'm

told the wrecks can still be seen lying on the bottom in the clear water.

Arriving late in the day, I took the last ferry from Narvik across the fiord to the northern side so I could get an early start on July 5th. It was a pleasure to be aboard the warm ferryboat as it rumbled across. It wasn't the scenery that appealed to me the most. The best part of that little ride was the toilet. A hitchhiker's bowels must be sufficiently disciplined to be active when the moment is right, and not any other time. From previous trips I had learned when a bathroom was available, that was the time to make use of it.

Much relieved, I debarked on the shore opposie Narvik and looked for a place to put up my tent until the first boat the next morning. Now what?

It was raining again. The gravel Arctic highway led up steeply into the mountains. Though there were some low, scrub trees, there was no woods, no flat ground anywhere to put up my tent. I struggled to get my heavy pack on my back and trudged laboriously up the grade looking for a spot.

All I could find that was flat  was a two track road going off someplace. I reasoned that since I had arrived on the last ferry from Narvik, there would be no northbound traffic until morning. Anyone who lived down that road, if they commuted to work, would not be using the road until morning. It was no more than two wet ruts, the only bit not awash being the hump in the middle.

Chilled by the Arctic cold, I set up the tent right in the middle of the road. If someone did come driving down it, they couldn't miss me. Miss seeing me if it was foggy, maybe, but not miss me.

It was a miserable night. I could not get warm. I woke up shivvering so much I could hardly dig out my candle and set it up in a cannister lid to light  for warmth. I sat, shaking with the cold, trying to warm my hands over the candle flame. A candle in a tent can warm it up several degrees. It helped but if I slept it was fitful, fearful that at any moment the blast of a truck horn would drive me out of the sack to frantically remove myself and my gear from the road before it was run over.

## Day Five: Friday, July 5, 1957

Hitchhiking at a ferry landing is always difficult, for there is no traffic until a ferry arrives. The ferry from Narvik to the road to the north ran every hour. I packed up early enough to meet the first one. After all, I didn't want to be in my tent in the middle of a road any longer than necessary.

Shouldering my pack, I trudged down the road to the ferry station, shopped to buy a few groceries, bought some postal cards, and waited expectantly for the arrival of the next batch of vehicles

Between arrivals, I shaved in the sea. It was a scramble to get down close enough to the shore and scoop up a cup of sea water from amidst the mess of weed. I discovered what every ocean seaman knows: soap will not lather in salt water. I did not

have shaving cream with me, just a bar of soap in an aluminum soap disk.

This was before Mr. Bic invented the disposable razor. My blades, always the cheapest available, felt like they had saw edges meant to grab and rip out the hairs on my face. It was a painful experience, but I felt I had to be clean shaven to get a lift. I might be a hobo, but I didn't want to look like one.

After three ferries came and went and no ride, I was beginning to get discouraged. Not much traffic flows north from Narvik. I wrote a few post cards and waited.

At last I got a lift a few miles further north to where the road split, one section westward to Tromsö, the other on to the far north.

I got a lift with a salesman who took me to a place on the coast, an intersection that led to the last ferry I would have to take before I got to Russenes. A ride got me to the ferry, but this one sailed only every two hours. All the cars taken aboard were too full of passengers and luggage to take me, too. It looked like I would be stuck again, this time with two hour intervals. Not good.

This ferry ride up the fjord was the most spectacular. The mountains on both sides were smoothed by ancient glaciers, solid rock going up hundreds of feet. Here and there ribbon-like waterfalls from the snow melting up top tumbled down the sides. I thought, what a wild ride it would be to go down one of those nearly vertical mountainsides on a sled, but of course at the bottom there was the sea.

Along the shore where there was a bit of nearly level land safe from avalanches there were occasional settlements, a building or two, a small dock if the water was shallow enough, but nothing more. Down between those high cliffs it would be difficult to pull in a radio signal and certainly no television. No coaxial cable served such remote places, and this was long before satellites were launched. Sputnik might send a peep-peep signal from its orbit, but TV communications satellites in stationary orbit 24,000 miles above the earth were the subject only for science fiction speculation. Anyone who lived alone those isolated shores could be reached only by boat. No roads were carved out of those steep, solid rock mountainsides.

It was cold. Why hadn't I expected to be so cold? After all, though it was July, this was the high arctic. And of course, it was never dark.

My sign for North Cape helped. As it rolled off the ferry a bus pulled up and I was beaconed aboard. I thought it was a commercial bus and they wanted a fare, something I feared might break my budget, but no, it was private and I was welcomed aboard for a free ride.

Their destination was Alta, not very far from my goal. I had not expected to get that far until the next day. But of course, it already was the next day. There is no distinguishing between day and night at that time of year in the arctic. Though the sun was hidden behind an overcast, it was always up; there was no morning, no afternoon, no night. As long as it was still light, one kept on driving. It was beyond midnight. In fact, we arrived at Alta at 4:30, not PM, but AM. Where they let me off was a couple of miles off the main road and I had to walk back, carrying my heavy knapsack. By the time I put up my tent and collapsed, exhausted, it was 5:30 in the morning.

## Sixth Day: Saturday, July 6, 1957

I slept until 10:00 but that was for less than four and a half hours. By now I was familiar with the weather pattern: clear and dry in the morning, then afternoon showers. I made breakfast and packed up before the rain put me back into my olive drab, rubberized US Army raincoat. It took two hours, waiting for the sparse traffic, before I got a lift to Skaldi, where the road split, left fork to Hammarfest, the right north to Russenes.

I was now in Lappland, and one can only be awed by the tenacity and courage of the Salmi, the Lapplanders. There, amidst melting snowfields, in icy rain, was a Salmi encampment. Skin tents and teepees of reindeer hides were the only shelter. So far north there is not a tree or even a bush. Everything was rock, soaked with rain, running with water from melting snow, with reindeer moss the fodder for the reindeer, the Lapps' primary source of food and material for clothing and shelter.

To compensate for the lack of color in the landscape, the Lapps wear brightly colored knit hats, skin boots trimmed with yellow, red and blue. One needs a bit of color in that windswept, raw arctic. I had never been in such a desolate, difficult place.

From Skaldi it was a short ride with some Finns who had never seen an American before and I arrived in Russenes, my rendezvous point. As is to be expected, there was not much there-- a few buildings, some docks for fishing boats, the ferry landing for the boat to Honningsvåg. On the outskirts, if such a small place could make that distinction, was a big frame structure like a warehouse without walls or a roof. You could smell it a long way off, and it attracted a flock of hungry gulls. It was a huge drying rack covered with worn out fishing nets. It wasn't for drying nets, though. It was for drying cod.

Here was the place where the infamous Lutefisk came from. I had seen the dried cod in the shops of Stockholm, big halves of rough, scaly fish that had to be soaked in brine to be reconstituted and turned into cooked Lutefisk, that traditional Christmas dish in Sweden.

I had tasted Lutefisk when we students at the International Graduate School had been invited for a typical Swedish festive meal, Lutefisk and risgrinsgröt. The rice pudding with the prize almond was delicious, but not lutefish. I found the sauce superior to the flesh which was flocculent like tripe or a cow's stomach, truly an acquired taste if one could ever get used to it at all. So this is where Lutefisk came from, split cod drying high on the racks, pooped on by seagulls unable to get inside the net barrier. Sometimes it's not good to know where your food comes from or how it is prepared.

The youth hostel in Russenes was unfinished, an unheated hut, but it had glass windows and a roof. Outside was a privy and a well. For a change I would sleep on a cot. The cot resembled what I'd slept on in Army basic training--some meager springs and a thin mattress, but compared to the hard, wet ground in the middle of a road outside Narvik or the gravel highway rest stop in pouring rain outside Trondheim it was luxury.

After six days on the road in a tent, I was ready for a real bed. I needed a rest. Long days with little sleep had worn me out. I could rest and do some laundry. Like the G I whose steel helmet was cooking pot, wash basin, and even latrine, my two liter aluminum pot had to serve many purposes. In this case it was to boil "hanky soup" the only way I could get handkerchiefs clean. I fired up the gasoline stove and boiled my handkerchiefs.

I waited for Jay and Lil Hutchinson to arrive. Would they make it?

Four Germans showed up at the hostel. They had taken three weeks to get to Russenes from Oslo. I had started in Stockholm and made it in only six days.

One tall, skinny German arrived by bicycle. I could not imagine traveling all that way on those gravel roads on a bicycle. He wore shorts in spite of the cold and his knees and legs were covered with scabs. He had started out with a friend but at one point they had been forced off the road into a ditch. This was before the days of bicycle helmets. Though he was badly cut up on the rocks, his friend had a concussion and had to be flown back to a hospital in Germany.

My hectic dash to the north was completed but I had not yet actually seen the midnight sun. If the rain stopped and the clouds ever broke I might. How long would I have to wait for Jay and Lil? Would they make it, or had they changed their minds? I would give them a day or two before giving up and going on alone to North Cape.

### Day Seven: Sunday, July 7, 1979

It took only a few minutes to walk through all of Russenes. Having done my meager laundry, I caught up on much needed sleep. One needs something to read, and I had been carrying a Penguin edition of Evelyn Waugh's "Officers and Gentlemen" which I finished reading. It was not as satisfying as "Scoop" or "Black Mischief" which were both great satires.

I wrote more postcards and was generally bored, hanging around the hostel hut and waiting for Jay and Lil.

New arrivals were two Frenchmen, a French girl, and two Norwegians. Sitting at a table and drinking beer, they had a lively discussion. It turned out that the young Frenchmen were royalists who believed in the return of the monarchy. They felt that the French resistance to the German occupation was a mistake, because for every German killed by the

Resistance, the Germans shot ten Frenchmen. The Norwegians disagreed.

I have never encountered royalist politics before, and thought the opinion an anachronism, but coming from a country that had abolished the monarchy I didn't get involved in the sometimes intense argument. France had an unstable government, with parliament dissolving whenever there was a vote of no confidence, and I could see that someone might see an advantage in the stability of a monarchy, but I merely listened in.

From July 1 to some time in August, the ferry Ingøy sailed between Honningsvåg to Russenes once a day, leaving Honningsvåg at noon, arriving at Russenes at 4:30, reloading and sailing back at 6:15 with arrival back north at 10:00 PM. The arrival and departure of the ship was the main event of the day. Excited, and wondering what the four hour passage would be like, I watched the arrival with some excitement. I wondered what sort of schedule they had the rest of the year. Surely in the long, sunless continuous dark of the Arctic winter there would be no boat traffic.

The weather, usually overcast and rainy, finally cleared. Sunshine at last. Birds must find it strange in the Arctic light, for when could they sleep? Since I had several days to become accustomed to the continuous daylight, I had little difficulty sleeping. It was just awkward wondering whether it was morning, afternoon, or the middle of the "night."

I napped and woke up at 11:00 PM. At least that's what my watch indicated. Though low on the horizon, the sun was still up. I walked down to the deserted, rocky shore, set up my twin-lens camera on the little tripod, and got into the self-timed photograph of the midnight sun. My goal had been accomplished.

## Day Eight: Monday, July 8, 1957

I had nothing to do all day but to wait for Jay and Lil. There's a little shop down at the ferry dock where I bought some postal cards and food, but there was little to choose from in the provision department. No fresh meat or vegetables, a few apples and a couple of oranges. They stocked some tinned goods like sardines or fiskebullar, fish balls, but I'd had my fill of those. I had nothing to read, having finished the Waugh book. One doesn't load a backpack with a big library!

At 6:00 PM I walked down to the dock to watch the ferry sail and, surprise, there were Jay and Lil. They had just arrived on the bus, hadn't even bothered to look for me, and would have sailed without me if I hadn't found them. I was pretty disappointed, having hurried my trip to make it to Russenes on time and then waited two days for them, but soon got over it.

It was too late for me to fetch my gear from the hostel and get back before the boat sailed. We would have to wait until the Tuesday boat. Jay and Lil didn't want to stay in the hostel hut, so I moved out and we set up our tents in the yard outside.

Though technically it was evening--who could tell without looking at a watch?-- we took a long walk, chatted with some Germans who had arrived pulling a trailer and a Dane who had actually come by bicycle. What a contrast: hauling a trailer across those mountains, through the tunnels, and on those treacherous gravel roads, compared with actually pedaling a bike.

Mountain bikes had not yet been invented. Though Raleigh in Nottingham, England made a three speed, most bicycles were single speed. Only racers and aficionados had multi-speed bikes with deraileurs. This was before the advent of 21 speed off-road bicycles with knobby tires and shock-absorbing suspensions. At least the Dane's bike was not a simple one speed, what the Brits call a "push bike" to distinguish them from a motorbike. It's an appropriate name, for a push bike is a bicycle one must push up all those gravel mountain grades. Thinking about the distances I had traveled and the rough terrain, I couldn't imagine bicycling from Denmark. It had been grim enough at times simply hitchhiking in the rain and cold.

In fine weather, Jay, Lil and I stood on a high hill overlooking the Bering Sea and watched the almost sunset as the sun sank closer and closer to the horizon, then began to rise again after midnight without ever disappearing. When one lives below the Arctic circle one doesn't fully appreciate the effect of the earth's wobble in its seasonal rotation. Sure, summer days are longer and sunset comes early in December, but back home in Indiana we did not have what the Russians in Leningrad call "white nights," the title of a book by Dostoyevsky.

We had seen the famed midnight sun, but we had not yet reached North Cape. For that we would have to wait another day and the next sailing of the Ingøy.

## Day Nine: Tuesday, July 9, 1957

If one has come so far to the Bering Sea, I would be a waste not go to swimming! Jay and I got into our bathing suits, walked down to the shore, and gingerly waded in. The beach was shingle, not sand, the sea bottom rocky, and the water frigid. I wish I could say that I actually swam, but I merely waded in up to my waist, ducked once in the the icy water and fled as fast as my bare feet could manage the stony bottom. We thought we might do better fishing and had some minimal fishing gear, some line and a few hooks, but we caught nothing.

When it came time for us to meet the ferry the German who had driven up to Russenes was kind enough to load our heavy packs in his car and drive us down to the dock for the 6:30 sailing. With a blast of its whistle, the Ingøy cast off.

That departing boat whistle is always exciting. One is embarking on a voyage, even though in this case it was only a few hours. We stood on deck as the ferry passed up the coast. Russenes is on the shore of Porsangerfjord and the ferry route goes along the coast in sheltered water. Up on the barren, rocky hillside we saw a herd of reindeer. The ship's captain blew the whistle, causing them to stampede. It was a thrilling sight to see all those galloping reindeer and we rumbled along the calm waters.

We docked in Honningsvåg and inquired about the bus to the cape itself. It would be leaving soon. The fare was 14 Norwegian kronor for the round trip. This was not an excursion one did on a one way ticket. The idea was to take the bus up to the cape, arriving about midnight, see the midnight sun, and return.

The view from the bus was like a moonscape, mountainous, rocky, with metallic-looking lakes like craters. The road wasn't paved, of course. Why pave something used so little?

Unfortunately, the weather changed. It had been overcast as we sailed up the fjord, but by the time the bus got to North Cape we were surrounded by a thick fog. Visibility was no more than a few yards and it was blowing hard. We could see nothing but the ground beneath our feet, gravel with some trampled vegetation. There was a little kiosk where one could buy a few postcards, a shop serving only a few bus passengers and probably open no more than an hour a day. What a disappointment!

We had come all the way to North Cape for the midnight sun and could see nothing but gray mist.

Jay and I decided if we had come that far, we should stay the night. Lil wasn't for it, so she got back on the bus to return to the town. Jay and I asked the driver if we could postpone our return for twenty-four hours. The driver, Kurt Jorgensen, wrote on the back of our tickets and signed the permission. "This person may ride back on this ticket. He will stay over one day."

(If you hold the picture to a mirror you can read the other side of the ticket.)

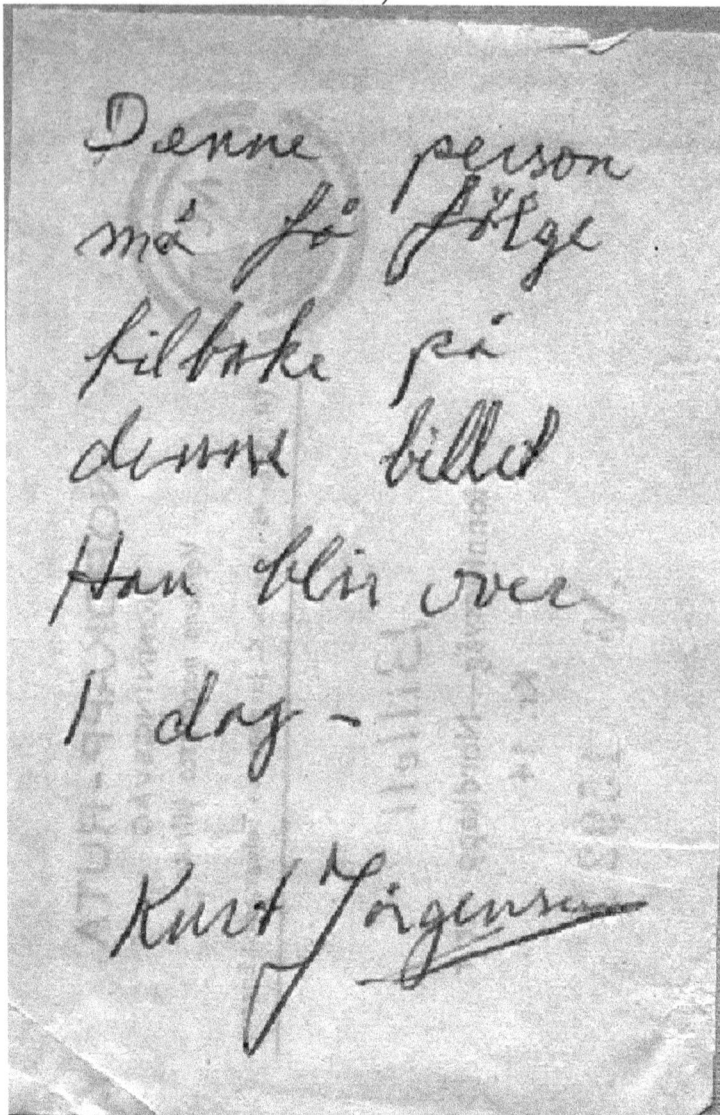

We could overnight, but where? The motor of the bus started up and the few quizzical passengers and Lil looked out the windows at us as the bus disappeared into the thick fog. How the driver would find the road in all that was a mystery. Whether we could find a place to put up my tent in the fog was a mystery, too.

The Arctic wind was fierce and cold as we set off  blindly in the thick fog, not knowing if we'd walk off the edge of a cliff. For all we knew, a down slope might just be the edge of a precipice. Eventually we came to a small ridge about two or three feet high that offered a small degree of shelter in its lee. Getting out every available bit of string and rope and all my metal tent pegs, I set up the tent and the fly sheet. With the fly sheet staked right onto the tundra with no gap under it, the wind was deflected over the top of the tent. I didn't think it would tear loose and blow us, inside the tent, into the unknown, but I wasn't sure.

The wind was about thirty or forty miles an hour and the tent ropes were strained. If the pegs didn't yank loose, the grommets might pull out. We would not know until morning where we were, providing the weather cleared. Putting our two double sleeping bags together as one, Jay and I were cozy and slept well.

## Day Ten: Wednesday, July 10, 1957

When we awoke, the fog was gone. We were not far from the edge of the cliff. The coastline and the surf thrown up against the cliffs are clear in this picture. It's a raw, inhospitable landscape.

If we had not stayed overnight in the tent we would not have seen any of this. Though the ground at the bus stop was bare, without a single flower, that was because tourists had picked everything for souvenirs or trampled them. Here, away from the road, the ground was covered with Arctic flowers that hugged the ground lest they be blown away.

We had not planned to stay overnight and didn't have much food. In Russenes I had only been able to buy rusks, no fresh bread or even Swedish hard tack. We had only one egg and some powdered milk between us. The solution was the mix up some milk, beat in the raw egg, and soak the rusks in it to fry French toast.

I set up my back pack upwind of the stove to give it some shelter so it wouldn't blow out, got it going, and with the stove hissing away in the shelter of the pack I cooked up all the French toast. We ate it with marmalade I'd packed in one of my screw-top aluminum containers. Frying a piece at a time for two people on that little stove took awhile but we were in no hurry. We had, after all, until midnight before the bus would return with the next crop of tourists. We dallied over breakfast for two hours.

After the stove was put away Jay and I went exploring. With no trees or obstructions to block our views from the top of North Cape, we could see in all directions, the rugged, wind-swept rocky islands and inlets. We tried to climb down to the water's edge but were stymied by a vertical drop to the sea.

That's Jay checking out the path to the dock below.

Working our way back up, we found a well-used path down to the water's edge. It was a long way down and at the bottom we found the body of a seal with the head missing. I wondered if a shark or killer whale had ripped it off. Scrambling back up the path to the top was exhausting, a steep climb of several hundred feet.

Here I am, Harley Sachs, Arctic explorer!

For supper, having run out of rusks, we cooked spaghetti Jay had carried along with some dehydrated gravy mix. A gourmet dinner it was not, but it was enough.

Then I sacked out while Jay, who had spotted some grouse, tried to pick one off by throwing stones. If he had succeeded we might have had a meal of fresh grouse, but he didn't come close.

From the edge of the cliff we had clambered down I saw a cruise ship. While we were hitchhiking and tenting in the rough, affluent tourists aboard a cruise ship had also come to see North Cape. Far down below, the white cruise ship looked like a bathtub toy, it was so far away. But they had no better luck seeing the midnight sun that we had, for as it grew later in the bright evening hours, the fog rolled in again. It was just as thick as it had been the night before.

To the surprise of the bus driver, we showed our endorsed tickets and got back on the bus to Honningsvåg. We were probably the only people he'd ever seen who actually camped overnight on the cape.

Back in town at about 1:00 in the "morning", the youth hostel was obviously locked up for the "night", so we spent the rest of the night on the ship. It would not sail until the next afternoon.

## Day Eleven: Thursday, July 11, 1957

We picked up Lil Hutchinson at the youth hostel. Since Jay had taken their double sleeping bag, she'd had to borrow a blanket. I realized that I needed to change the way I loaded my knapsack and I needed a couple of leather straps. We found a camping supply store and bought a couple. Now, instead of carrying my tent by the handle on its case I could strap it underneath my pack. Ideally, a knapsack should put weight high on the shoulders, not on the back. Though the Boy Scout knapsack was small, with the sleeping bag as a U shaped sausage over the top and with the tent underneath it, bumping my bottom with every step, my load was pretty big and cumbersome. The used frame I had bought in Stockholm helped some, but it was makeshift at best.

Farewell, North Cape!

I felt a little like those mountain climbers who, having reached the summit, now faced the long return trip. For mountaineers, that is often the most dangerous part of an expedition. They are tired, may be in a hurry, and make mistakes. In my case, I was returning to Stockholm, but not by the same route. I had never been in northern Finland.

Once back in Russenes in mid "afternoon," Jay and Lil placed themselves on the north side of the road, hitchhiking west, with me on the south side heading east toward Finland. They soon got a lift. We would not meet again until the next year, as it would turn out, for they moved on from student status in Sweden to a job in Madrid, Spain.

I was alone again. Now I needed a new sign, one that said "Stockholm." There is little traffic in the high Arctic, but after a two hour wait along came a Kaiser-Frazer compact car, one of the first American compacts. It was driven by a Finn who, with his son, was heading for Rovaniemi, a two day drive.

The Finn didn't speak any Swedish, German or English, so we had to communicate by sign language, with me showing my map and he, after some hesitation and study, pointing out his destination. A two day lift. What luck! Having been stuck for hours on the Norwegian coast and sometimes gotten short rides that dropped me at some deserted, uninhabited intersection, a two day lift to a city was terrific.

That corner of Norway is the only part with a border on the Soviet Union. The gravel road was rough, the stones as big and sharp as railway ballast, but we were on our way and soon across the Finnish border! The Kaiser-Frazer two-door car was a noisy, tin box of a car. We traveled through endless tundra and Arctic forest, the trees on either side of the road. This was not the massive rain forest one sees in mild climates, but trees with a short growing season and harsh conditions. Finland is a land of forests, lakes, and mosquitoes. We rumbled along, miles and miles though the woods.

When the Finnish driver was tired of driving he pulled off beside a rushing river to make camp. He and his son had a tent and we all searched for places among the big rocks and trees for a place flat enough and dry enough to set up camp.

If the mosquitoes at Kongsvinger were bad, these were the kind that drive the reindeer insane. I had to tuck my khaki pants in my socks and wrap my GI towel over my head like a Moslem to keep them off my ears and neck. Ravenous, a dozen at a time would land on the back of my hand. The stick of bug dope I had been given by one driver had no effect. Setting up my stove to cook had to be done quickly.

The driver who had given me a lift didn't have much food with him , so I opened a packet of dehydrated soup, added water from my canteen, cooked up a potful which we all shared. It was the least I could do to return the favor of a lift.

Getting into the tent without being accompanied by a squadron of mosquitoes took all my camping skills. I'd never seen mosquitoes as bad as that anywhere. They say a deer can lose enough blood, standing in those clouds of insects, to actually keel over and die.

### Day Twelve: Friday, July 12, 1957

I was up before my host driver. I had a couple of eggs which I fried up for my breakfast, but my host and his son were not prepared. I speculated about this man. Where had he come from? Why was he so ill prepared? Though I was living out of a knapsack, I always tried not to run out of provisions because I knew I sometimes wouldn't have a chance to buy any food. My host had a tent, of course, but I wondered where was his wife? In Rovaniemi, perhaps. That was his destination.

Rovaniemi, Finland is just south of the Arctic circle. I got a quick lift to the southern edge of town. I was wearing my now rather soiled, originally white Swedish student cap and was surprised when a Finnish soldier in uniform saluted me. Maybe it was a joke. After only a fifteen minute wait at the edge of

Rovaniemi I was picked up by a lumber truck that took me all the way to the Swedish border at Haparanda.

Haparanda is a lumber town on the frontier. Sweden and Finland are separated there by Tornealv, a rushing, shallow, rocky river typical of northern streams fed by melting snow. The Tornealv runs into the Gulf of Bothnia, an arm of the Baltic sea which separates Sweden from Finland.

The border crossing was not much more than a hut manned by a couple of bored agents. I do not think they saw many hikers with back packs, certainly not Americans. I dug out my passport from its protective plastic bag and cleared the pass control. Again, of course, it wasn't stamped.

It was late in the day. Now that I was south of the Arctic it was actually warm. It was the first warm day I had experienced the entire trip. In Norway I had been poorly dressed for the wind and the cold. Now it actually felt like summer. What a relief!

I carried my gear down to the bank of the river, set up the tent, cooked dinner on the gasoline stove and went to bed early. I was tired from the long ride down to Rovaniemi and then being shaken on the lumber truck. Neither had been very comfortable, but I had made a great distance in only three lifts. I was ahead of schedule.

Schedule? You'd think a wanderer like me had no schedule at all, especially now that the meeting with Jay and Lil Hutchinson and the North Cape bit was over. The remainder of the summer lay ahead of me. I was half way through July. August beaconed. Classes at the International Graduate School would not start again until September, and with them the resumption of the Gi Bill checks. I would be solvent again, able to pay rent, and have to find a new place to live, but in the meantime, I shouuld be free of schedules.

Ah, but I had made arraangements to meet a friend, Ingrid Henning, at her father's home in Härnosand. She was in Stockholm and after visiting her father and sisters in northern Sweden, she planned to hitchhike with me to see her boy friend in Paris.

Ingrid and I were friends. We didn't date and there was no romance involved. Several of us hung around together, went to parties, enjoyed each other's company. I guess she felt that even if we shared the same sleeping bag I was a safe guy, harmless, affable, and a suitable partner for a hitchhiking jaunt to France.

I had arranged to pick up Ingrid on the 16th of July and here it was only the twelfth. It would not take four days to get to her family's place. I did not want to arrive in Härnosand too soon.

### Day Thirteen: Saturday, July 13, 1957.

I got a late start on Saturday morning and then had bad luck. I'd read about the shopping center in Luleå, which was not very far away, but in Sweden the shops closed at noon on Saturday and remained closed all weekend. I got a lift from some Finns, but by the time I arrived in Luleå the shops were closed. They would not reopen until Monday.

In fact, nothing would be open on Sunday except the occasional bakery where one could buy fresh baked rolls. This was Scandinavia where one valued a day off, not the USA where stores will stay open 24/7 if customers will come in. I had to press on.

I was impressed by the generosity of Finnish drivers. Perhaps it is a sense of mutual struggle to survive in the north. Swedes tended to be smug and conservative, possibly because auto insurance constraints made them liable if a passenger were hurt. Finns were friendlier, willing to made room for me even if their small cars were already cramped.

Some Finns gave me a lift which proved helpful because they made a couple of stops. Somewhere along the line I had lost my ball point pen, and at their first stop I was able to buy another. More important, at their second stop I was able to replenish my diminished sack of victuals.

When hitchhiking one is at the mercy of the elements and the whims of the drivers. A hitchhiker is a guest, after all, and can't say, "Stop here. I want to buy a loaf of bread." One never knows when the next opportunity to shop will be.

For a change, I had to stay in a bona fide campground, fee one Swedish crown, about twenty-five cents. I had not stayed in any campgrounds on the whole trip, for there weren't many and if I got a ride I stayed with it as far as I could. That meant camping rough wherever I could find a place to put up the tent. The Swedish campground was luxurious by comparison. Even though the water was barely warm and trickled, I could take a shower, do some laundry, and even give myself a haircut. I had never met Ingrid Henning's family and had to be presentable.

## Day fourteen: Sunday, July 14, 1957

I left the campground about 9:00 AM on that quiet Sunday morning.The Swedish campground was well off the main road. Since my pack weighed about fity or sixty pounds, carrying it was difficult. Even with the pack frame, the straps cut into my shouldlers and the tent, tied under the pack with the leatherstraps I'd bought in Honningsvåg kept banging against my butt. I just had to hang onto the straps to take some of the weight off my shoulders and soldier on. Stopping frequently to rest, I had to walk a couple of miles before I reached the highway where I could get a ride.

Once there I made good time. Between about 10:30 AM and 7:00 PM I covered about 180 miles, not bad for a quiet Sunday in Sweden. I got the longest lift from a friendly jeepload of Finns. I had seen their jeep before on the road. This time they decided to pick me up. They were were already so crowded that there was no place for my pack. I had to take off my belt and use it to lash the pack to the radiator, fearing that if it came loose the jeep would run over it and rip everything to shreds. I posed for a picture, sans belt, as a souvenir of that remarkable ride.

They were good humored folks and though their Swedish was minimal we laughed a lot. I was picking up that characteristic Finnish accent.

The Finns took me as far as Umeå and in another twelve miles I got to a tiny woods where I camped. It was about a quarter of a mile off the main road, barely a corner of a fallow field with a few trees. I set up my tent but discovered that, while northern Finland has clouds of mosquitoes, this place had swarms of pesky flies.

My food supply included some chunks of meat, potatoes, and carrots I'd been carrying for awhile, and the meat was getting a bit ripe, perfect bait for flies. If I didn't cook it at once, by the next day it would have to be thrown away. In order to cook my supper, I had to set up the gasoline stove outside the tent. Putting the ingredients in my aluminum pot to make a stew, I kept waving the flies away, but they kept flying into the fragrant steam as the stew boiled.

Finally, unable to stand the flies any longer, I shut off the stove and retreated into the tent to eat out of the pot. Inside the tent it was pretty dark, and I'd eaten much of my stew before I realized that not all the ingredients were things I had put in. Some of the flies, overcome by the steam, had fallen in and been cooked, too. There was no telling how many flies I had eaten along with the meat, potatoes and carrots, but they were cooked and shouldn't make me sick. I hoped.

### Day Fifteen: Monday, July 15, 1957

The very thought of having to deal with those darned flies drove me out of my camp site without breakfast the next day. I just had to get out of there. By 7:00 AM I was back out on the road and made very good time, soon arriving in Härnosand where I was to pick up Ingrid Henning and continue on to Paris.

I had misgivings about meeting her family. It wasn't that I didn't know how her father would react to his daughter going off hitchhiking with a strange American guy, but because, after fifteen days on the road, in spite of being able to shower and do some essential laundry at the Swedish campground, I was pretty filthy and rough.

Härnosand was a pretty, quiet town on the Baltic coast with the usual yellow stucco buildings and typical signs for bakeries, barbers, and the like. Those signs have ancient origins. While in the United States a barber's striped pole is the icon for those services, in Sweden it's the crescent-shaped metal plate that fits behind the neck while someone gets a shampoo. A pretzel-shaped sign indicates a bakery, and several iron balls, similar to what pawn brokers use in the US, mark a hardware store.

I had Ingrid Henning's phone number and found a phone booth but no one answered. I didn't want to schlep my heavy pack around town,. After asking directions for the address I found the Henning house, a big, old frame structure that was almost American in that it had a front porch. I left my pack on the porch with a note saying I'd soon be back.

I had some chores to do, like go a bank and exchange money. In spite of my appearance, I went to a restaurant and had a decent meal for a change, wienerschnitzel with potatoes and vegetables. It had been awhile since I had freshly cooked vegetables. At least this meal didn't include boiled flies! Not that the Norwegian fried fish balls were that appetizing, either.

I wrote a few more post cards and returned to the Henning house.

My note had been replaced by one of theirs. I had written in my rudimentary Swedish, but the response was in fluent English, saying the Mr. Henning was painting the roof. No wonder no one had answered my knock at the door!

Mr. Henning turned out to be a teacher who was well versed in languages, particularly Latin. He also brewed his own aquavit, which he pressed upon me. We were like a pair of old friends. All my trepidation about not being welcomed in the Henning household evaporated in a cloud of well-being lubricated by the Henning home brew.

I think it's a Swedish sport to get a guest drunk. The typical menu included an appetizer of aquavit, served in a conical glass and tossed down so it hit the throat, not the tongue. It was followed by wine during dinner and brandy afterwards for a cumulative effect. That was the routine when Sven Huldt and his wife Ray had invited me to dinner. I have seldom been drunk, but that dinner with the Hennings was one of those occasions.

What I did learn, before being steered to a bed in a small guest room, was that my friend Ingrid wasn't coming. The hitchhiking trip to Paris was off. That disappointment was quickly dispelled by her sister Åse's declaration that she would like to hitchhike with me, not to Paris, but to Nice in the south of France.

Nice, on the Mediterranean coast, is a renowned vacation spot. It was a long way. To get there we'd pass through Denmark, Germany, Switzerland and southern France. Having been stationed in Heidelberg, I had friends there from the fencing club, and a friend from Indiana University, an opera singer, was currently in Munich so there were stops to make along the way. When Åse got her affairs in order, she'd meet me in Stockholm and we'd hitchhike to Nice.

Mr. Henning by now considered me practically a member of the family and approved. Åse was younger and prettier than her sister Ingrid and a lithe gymnast. Who knew how that trip might develop? Ah, those bachelor's fantasies!

Mr. Henning, Åse, her sister, and Harley

I was not only a welcomed guest, but a pampered one. Without commenting on the condition of my grubby khakis, Åse offered to do my laundry. I was soon stripped and wrapped, embarrassed, in a borrowed bathrobe while all my wardrobe went into the Henning washing machine. Åse even ironed my pants.

So far as I knew, there was no Mrs. Henning. Mr. Henning not only made his own aquavit recipe, but he had specific instructions on how to prepare rhubarb he brought in from their garden. He specified exactly how many decileters of sugar were to go into the pot, but once he left the room Åse just cooked it up to her taste. I doubt if he ever knew the difference.

What I had feared might be a rebuff when I showed up at the Henning home turned into a warm-hearted welcome and a happy experience.

I didn't know when the trip to Germany and France might take place. In the meantime, I had to continue on my trip back to Stockholm.

### Day sixteen: Tuesday, July 16, 1957

I was used to getting up early and hitting the road, but did not want to rush off so quickly. I was up early enough to chat with the athletic Åse before she left to play tennis. I hung around until after lunch and she accompanied me on her bicycle down to the main road where we chatted until I got a lift.

It was the last day of my Arctic adventure. I got rides quickly, Härnosand, Sundsvall, Gävle, and on to Stockholm. My last ride was with a Coca-Cola execuvie and ended at Ängby campground. By then it was too late to call my friends and mooch a place to crash until Åse was ready to join me and hitchhike south. I paid the 1.5 kronor fee, about 25 cents, to camp.

Kvitto
Kronor 1:50 № 19878

å erlagd tältplatsavgift
för den _____ 195___
(gäller från kl. 12 ovanstående dag
till kl. 12 påföljande dag)

Tältnr                    Tältinnehavare

Stockholms stads idrotts- och friluftsstyrelse

LIDHSTRÖMS TR.

The campground was crowded. European campgrounds are not like those in the United States where every space has a picnic table and a fire pit, perhaps even an electrical hookup with a water tap nearby. European campgrounds do have central toilet and shower buildings, but no tables and no fires. Tents may be so close together than passing between them means doing a skip and hop to avoid tripping over the guy ropes. I had to search for a space among the hundreds of tents.

My language skills were improving. In high school I had failed Latin but eventually got a B. In college I had begun by failing German, but caught on and eventually got a B in conversation and even made the language my minor, a fluke that in the army got me stationed in Germany instead of Korea. At the International Graduate School I began with a C in basic Swedish, but I had an ear for the sounds of language. Once I had learned enough vocabulary to think in the language, I made rapid progress.

Swedes I met at the Stockholm campground thought I was from northern Sweden. I must have picked up an accent talking with the Hennings. I'd only been in Sweden less than a year, so if my Swedish was good enough for me to be mistaken for a native from northern Sweden, I was making good progress, indeed!

In spite of the cold, the wet, and the frequent exhaustion, the North Cape trip had been a great adventure. What would be next? The lovely Åse Henning off with me to the south of France? Would her sister Ingrid and I ever make it to Paris? There was no telling.

At the end of the month I tallied up my expenses. For the trip to North Cape I had spent all of $35, about two dollars a day. At that rate my meager savings would easily last until the G.I. Bill checks resumed in September.

What I didn't know was that in a few weeks my carefree life would come to an end. This had been a happy interval. There were other adventures ahead, but they had a dark side. That's a different story.

## About Harley L. Sachs:

Though born in Chicago and raised in Indiana, Harley L. Sachs considers himself an international, having lived in Germany, Sweden, Scotland, and Denmark. He earned a degree in English at Indiana University, then served in the US Army in Germany. After getting his Master's degree at I.U. he returned to Europe and worked under cover for several years. He met and married Ulla in Stockholm, Sweden and they spent a year's honeymoon in a Scottish castle. Returning to the USA, Sachs taught English briefly at Southern Illinois University then moved to Michigan Technological University in the Upper Peninsula where he and his wife raised three daughters. He took early retirement and now lives in Portland, Oregon.

If you enjoyed this Harley Sachs memoir there are others. The honeymoon mentioned in the author's bio is written up as *From Tent to Castle: Memoir of a Year Long Honeymoon.*

## Here's a sample:

**Foreword: The Fog of Memory**

Memory is elusive. We are all familiar with the general terms long term and short term memory. Short term memory enables us to remember a phone number we have looked up in the directory and keep it long enough to dial it; then we forget it. Long term memory seems to be burned indelibly into our brains to last forever. Unfortunately, memory is malleable. At a science lecture we were once passed a bit of fragile foam to examine. As it went around the room it got smaller and smaller until at last it crumbled away altogether. Though each person who touched it examined he same substance, its shape and size were changed by every handler. Had it been a bit of soft clay it might not have lost its mass, but its shape would surely have changed. The same applies to memory.

A memory examined or recollected is changed by the act of recollection. The imagination embellishes memory, fills in the gaps. A caught fish grows bigger with the retelling of the story. There are also false memories, memories altered by our imagination. Things that may never have happened become real. For an author who imagines and creates vivid characters and puts them down on paper, the paper record is stable, but the memory of what was imagined changes over time. A character imagined by an author for a story may be more vivid to him than a real person he has met. Hence Balzac, on his deathbed, called out for the doctor he had created for his opus "The Human Comedy" as if that character had been real.

We also forget. Were it not for the diaries I kept over the years, this memoir would not be possible, but in using the diaries and their journal entries as a touchstone, I realize how much I have forgotten in the forty-plus years that have transpired since these events happened. Day to day activities and trivia do not set in long term memory, and long term memory itself changes with the reexamination. It is like trying to mold a statue out of fog.

Someone who does not keep a diary or record in any manner the events of his life lives mainly in the present. The past is elusive. Memories are lost entirely or are altered to a fantasy fiction. The future is a mystery, the past history, and the present is a present, a gift of transient life gone in a flash.

This memoir of a single year in our lives is an attempt to recall and preserve a passage that otherwise will surely be lost forever.

-- Harley L. Sachs, summer, 2004

Even if you don't choose to read the honeymoon memoir, there are many more books by Harley L. Sachs. Take a look!

Here's a list of other books by Harley L. Sachs:

## MYSTERY NOVELS

### The Mystery Club Series

THE MYSTERY CLUB SOLVES A MURDER
First and most popular of the Mystery Club series. Mary Higgins finds the body of Dora Reed on the roof of the Plaza retirement building, notifies the police, then tells the Mystery Club. They assume several suspects: the manager of the Plaza, Dora's son Donald, or a Plaza employee. Dora's husband, Ed Sutherland, is in Hawaii on board the yacht Miss Chief with an all girl crew. Carrying on their

own investigation, the Mystery Club finally suspects Sutherland, though he seems to have a perfect alibi. If they can prove it to their satisfaction, will a court ever convict him-- if he can be found somewhere in the Pacific?

## THE MYSTERY CLUB AND THE DEAD DOCTOR
Second in the Mystery Club series. The Mystery Club consists of five elderly women who live at the Rose Plaza and discuss mysteries written by women. The Mystery Club ladies have no idea of the consequences when Viola Cartwright, their blind member, asks them to go over her Medicare bills. That leads to suspicion about the identity of her personal assistant, Dorothy Anderson, who turns out to be using a stolen identity. Viola's doctor runs a phony clinic owned by a member of the Russian Mafia. Soon the investigation of Medicare bills leads to murder and tragedy, stopped only by the courage of Mary Higgins.

## THE MYSTERY CLUB AND THE HIDDEN WITNESS
Third in the Mystery Club series. The ladies of the Mystery Club discover one of the residents is a crook under WITSEC, the witness protection program. He apparently keeps dipping into the employee gift fund. The Mystery Club bands together to track down the missing money, but what they discover is danger.

## THE MYSTERY CLUB AND THE SERIAL WIDOW
Fourth in the Mystery Club series. Caroline Kostinsky, new resident at the Rose Plaza, is a widow four times over and she's looking for a fifth husband in retired General Hardcastle, but when drunk she says she killed all of her husbands. Except for her confession, there's no evidence. Now what?

## DELIVER ME FROM EVIL
Responding to a posted invitation for new members for the Mystery Club, Judge Ira Kahane and Ursula Besette show up. Ursula, at a turning point in her life as a new Rose Plaza resident, is interested in Wicca and Kabala. Roberta Nelson believes one should not suffer a witch to live.

Judge Kahane tries to lead Ursula on the right path, but there is conflict and tragedy coming.

## WHITE SLAVE

Sequel to *The Mystery Club Solves a Murder.* The appearance of Ed Sutherland's gold bracelet in a Portland pawn shop revives retired detective Casey's interest in the cold case. He doesn't know that Sutherland has been picked up and is a slave on a Korean fishing boat. Sutherland, penniless, .without clothes or identification, is stranded in New Zealand. Can he find his way back to Portland and be somehow redeemed or face a death sentence for first degree murder?

# The Irwin Glass Series

## BETRAYAL

Prequel to *Retribution.* Irwin Glass, BA in Russian, MA in International Relations, has a promising career in the Foreign Service in Moscow until he is snared in a classic "honey pot" seduction. He's young and naïve, honest, always wants to do the right thing, but at every turn he is betrayed. The incident in Moscow destroys his career. He is accused of being a paid Soviet agent and is pursued by the consequences of his encounter with the KGB twenty years later. Some enemies never let go

## RETRIBUTION

Sequel to *Betrayal.* Newly married to Ivy Hartshorn, Irwin Glass gets a dunning letter from the IRS for taxes on interest at the Washington, DC account he didn't think he had. It's a joint account with his missing birth daughter and the balance is huge. Assuming it's money Katya's KGB father of record, Vladimir Putinsky (now Putin) deposited for her living expenses, Irwin moves it to force her to contact him. But Ivy warns him that he is laundering money and the people it belongs to will come after him. Irwin's complicated life is catching up with him, but this time he will find retribution.

## BURNT OUT
Irwin Glass is approached by FBI Agent Wilkins who asks for Irwin's lists of foreign students. Not satisfied he wants more and is looking for potential terrorists among the Moslem students. Gradually Irwin is sucked into the role of FBI informant on the Michigan Institute of Technology's Muslim Students' Association and the results are tragic.

## OTHER MYSTERIES

### MURDER BY MAIL
German exchange student Klaus Hitz is more interested in making money than in asking questions about his work assignment. He doesn't know that the industrialist father of his punk girl friend is using him in a terrorist conspiracy to kill everyone in the United States with a mass mailing of a scratch and sniff virus. The plot begins to unravel when a Polish nurse brings blood samples from Libya and alerts a CIA agent. While the CIA and FBI track down the terrorists, Klaus Hitz gradually figures it out. How can he avoid being murdered or imprisoned for being naive?

### MURDER IN THE KEWEENAW
CIA agent recovering from Post traumatic Stress after failed missions in Finland and a divorce is fishing in Lake Superior when he snags a corpse. He thinks he has seen the girl before and his attempt to identify her leads him to a ring of deadly pornographers. It almost costs him his own life.

### CONSPIRACY!
Technical writer Tom Godot can't believe his luck when CONSPIRACY!, the book he has co-written with the elusive Harold Stevenson, is a hit. The book details a plot to hijack communication satellites. As Tom crosses the country on his book tour, he is disturbed by people interested in early drafts and dogged by an NSA agent. Communicating by fax with his editor and by encrypted e-mail with the mysterious Stevenson, Tom reaches out in his loneliness to his California girl friend Sylvia Hanson who

Harley L. Sachs 76

turns out to be a pivotal figure.     There is another conspiracy, and Tom is part of it

## THE GOLD CHROMOSOME

When Adam Rottman's childless Aunt Sadie Gold died, the eight cousins learned her estate was in an irrevocable trust, the proceeds going to Adam's sister Sarah while she lives. After Sarah's death, the money would go to the last surviving cousin.  It's a fatal tontine Adam's lawyer brother Harold set up.   Would the cousins kill each other for one million dollars? Sarah's car is found in the river, but not Sarah.     That begins a series  of mysterious deaths. Coincidence? Or Murder? Who will be next? Adam and his psychologist wife Deborah must stop the chain before he, too, is eliminated.

## BEN ZAKKAI'S COFFIN

Born of a Jewish father and a Catholic mother, Herman Bachrach insists he has no religion, but he is drawn by circumstance into a holocaust vendetta over gold stolen by a Swiss bank from Jewish depositors.     Seduced by a woman who calls herself Diana, no last name, Herman is suspected by detective Sheehan to be her murderer. Someone else wants him dead.   His Jewish boss provides him with a lawyer, but sends him to Switzerland to finish the job "Diana" started.   It's an assignment he can't refuse. The result is an epiphany of identity that changes Herman's life forever.

## THE LOLLIPOP MURDER

A warning for wannabe novelists! What happens when a stable of neurotic novelists who live in their pseudonyms and are bound by iron clad contracts are invited aboard their miserly Florida publisher's yacht for the Miami Book Fair only to find that they have no hope of ever earning a dime of royalties for their books? All this as Hurricane Gerta threatens to sink the yacht at the dock.   It's grounds for murder

## SCI-FI AND FANTASY

## NEVER TRUST A TALKING HORSE

The narrator of this dystopian novel escapes preventive detention into a world he discovers has gone mad. Hungry, he is told he can eat for free at Lachumba's supper club, only to discover that he might be the main dish. He rescues Iris I. Iris from the ovens and in a series of episodes explores the insane world in search of a livelihood. He gradually realizes why he was incarcerated in the first place, but by then it is too late. His and Iris's roles have been reversed. Arrested, they are given a sadistic sentence which is their final challenge.

## THE SEARCH FOR JESSE BRAM

Jesse Bram, the young hero of this metaphysical science fiction adventure, is unaware of his Jewish roots. An Eldre of mixed breed, he is marooned on the post apocalyptic shunned planet URth where technology and books have been destroyed. The URthlings variously view Jesse as a bringer of cargo for the half-breed prefect Hrod, as the reborn Savior by crypto-Christians, and as a link to the past by a remnant of Jews. The Galactic Federation suspects him of treason and he is pursued by an enigmatic Trinian policeman. If Jesse survives, will he be convicted? If acquitted, what next?

## A ROMANCE NOVEL

## SAM IN LOVE

U.S. Army life in Europe in the 1950's was an equivalent of the Grand Tour of the eighteenth century when young men traveled and sowed wild oats. Marty, roommate of Sam Logan, a PFC draftee serving in the US Army in Munich, Germany, says all Sam needs is to get laid. Sam is not a virgin, but has a Midwestern ethic and believes in love. He doesn't know quite what that is. No Casanova, Sam, through a series of tentative encounters, thinks he's found the love of his life.

# SHORT STORIES

## THREADS OF THE COVENANT: THE JEWS OF RED JACKET
A collection of twenty-one short stories about Jewish life in small town America centering about two main characters, David Katz, the only Jewish boy in Red Jacket, and Richard Goldman, the only Jewish professor at Copper country Community College. Each story depicts another aspect of what it means to be a Jew in a small town as each character comes to realize his own identity.


## MISPLACED PERSONS
Though set in different locales what these stories have in common is a central character who is out of his element, in the wrong place, coming to grips with cultural, generational, or physical displacement.    In PROBLEM FOR THE TEACHER an expatriate fumbles for a living; in LIMBO an ex-G.I.  is adrift in Copenhagen; in TRIUMPH OF THE WILL a nervous wreck seeks recuperation; in MISCALCULATION a would be tax evader succumbs to his own fears; in THE LIE a drunk gets himself into difficulties, and in THE GIRLS OF FREDERIKSHAVN an old man is trapped by girls looking for action.

## YOOPER TALES AND OTHER FUNNY STUFF
Extracted from the massive volume of Sachs's published Essays and Columns: 1992-2011, this collection of stories related to Michigan's Upper Peninsula, known as the UP, home of Yoopers, reveals the truth about snow fleas, ice worms, the humungous fungus (world's largest living thing) and the rigors of winters in the remote north woods. You can also learn how to catch and cook the Mosquito Giganticus and why visitors won't come. Sachs has several awards for his humor.

## AHOY! QUARTERDECK!
Originally published as IRMA QUARTERDECK REPORTS but re-released with new illustrations and, in the

paperback edition, with sea shanties, this funny book is a series of boating anecdotes about Irma and her bumbling husband Ralph ("I can't believe I lost the anchor") Quarterdeck in their many boating adventures and mishaps. One reviewer says the book is as informative as Chapman's famous manual, but more fun. Readers will find plenty of laughs in this book and at the same time learn a great deal of boating fundamentals.

ANNA-LENA'S TROLL AND OHER STORIES
Each of the three Sachs daughters has a story in this children's book. "Anna-Lena's Troll" explores the nature of trolls, which represent the dark side of human behavior as Anna-Lena's nasty letter to Santa is rewarded by the gift of a nasty troll. "The Return of Baby Suzy" is the true story of Cynthia's worn out doll and its resurrection. "The Stars for Christmas" is the remarkable surprise Belinda got along with her new eye glasses. Other family stories are Christmas related.

## NON-FICTION

THE MISADVENTURES OF CPL. SACHS
Adrift through college at Indiana University, author Sachs was drafted at the end of the Korean War. Physically unfit for combat, he was sent to Queer Company for basic training, then by a fluke was shipped out to Germany instead of Korea. Thus began his own version of the traditional Grand Tour.

FREELANCE NONFICTION ARTICLES
This third edition of a monograph on freelance writing first published by the Society for Technical Communication is newly updated. This little manual provides tips for interviewing, article structure, article preparation and submission, photography, and business practice.

CHILLY-CHILLY-BANG—HOW WE FREELANCED THROUGH EUROPE'S COLDEST WINTER IN A VW WITH A KID

Companion piece to *Freelance Nonfiction Articles*. The former is a how to book. This is a "how we did it" memoir. The author knew nothing about Volkswagens when they set off, but as they worked from VW dealer to dealer getting the old Combi fixed, he learned! It's as much a book for VW enthusiasts as it is for writers.

Both FREELANCE NONFICTION ARTICLES and *Chilly-Chilly-BANG! How we Freelanced Through Europe's Coldest Winter in a VW with a Kid* are combined in a double volume, *The Writing Life*.

THE 1957 SACHS ARCTIC EXPEDITION
After military service in Germany the author took the GI Bill to Sweden. With no income in the summer, and not even sure there was a road to the far north, he set off hitchhiking to North Cape, the northernmost point in Europe in search of the midnight sun. Illustrated.

FROM TENT TO CASTLE: MEMOIR OF A YEAR LONG HONEYMOON
Setting off from Stockholm, Sweden on rebuilt one speed bicycles, Harley and Ulla embarked on an open-ended honeymoon with no fixed destination and equipped with a tent, a thin double sleeping bag, a tiny gasoline stove, and $3000. After arriving in Britain, Ulla discovered she was pregnant. Tired of unrelenting rain, they advertised for a cheap place to spend the winter. They were offered the gatehouse to Borthwick Castle outside Edinburgh, Scotland for $25 a month by British author Theo Lang.

"IS"
As Bill Clinton said, "It all depends on what the meaning of "is" is."
A problem we all have is distinguishing between what is real and what is not. This is in fact an age-old question. This volume switches between classical instances of the problem to the author and his psychiatrist and his wife. What is real? That all depends on the meaning of "real."

QUEER COMPANY

Not a gay novel, this is a fictionalized memoir of an experimental basic training unit at the end of the Korean War. All the draftees were physically unfit for combat but the army didn't want to discharge them. Instead they got modified training in a company unfortunately designated Q. In the Army phonetic alphabet Q is Queen, but Q company was called queer. A copy is in the US Army historical archives.

www.ingramcontent.com/pod-product-compliance
Lightning Source LLC
Chambersburg PA
CBHW031330040426

42443CB00005B/282